CLAY PLAY

Ed Catherall

Wayland

Science is Fun

Balls and Balloons
Clay Play
Colours
Floating and Sinking
Fun with Magnets
Fun with Wheels
Growing Plants
Light and Dark
Our Pets
Sand Play

Illustrations by David Anstey

First published in 1985 by
Wayland (Publishers) Ltd
49 Lansdowne Place, Hove
East Sussex BN3 1HF, England

ISBN 0 85078 583 9

Phototypeset by
Kalligraphics Ltd, Redhill, Surrey
Printed in Italy by
G. Canale & C.S.p.A., Turin
Bound in the U.K. by
The Bath Press

CONTENTS

Clay play

Find some clay to play with.
Feel your clay.
Is it hard or soft?
Is it warm or cold?

Squeeze your clay.
What do you feel?
Does the clay stain your fingers?
Keep squeezing the clay.
How many squeezes does it take before
your clay is warm and soft?

Size and shape

Take two different-sized balls of clay.
Make a different shape from each ball of clay.
Ask your friends which shape is bigger.
Roll each shape back into a ball to prove
which shape is bigger.

Make different solid shapes such as cubes,
cubiods, cylinders and pyramids.

Cuboid

Pyramid

Cylinder

Cube

Making a clay snake

Take a ball of soft clay.
Notice the size of this ball of clay.

Roll the ball on a smooth board to make a snake.
How long can you make this snake?
What happens if you try to make the snake longer?

Roll your snake back into a ball.
What do you notice about the size of this clay ball?

Making clay tiles

Place a large soft ball of clay on a smooth board.
Use a rolling pin to roll out the clay
to form a flat tile.

Cut the tile into different shapes with a plastic knife.
Make a square, a rectangle and a triangle shape.
Make shapes with curved edges such as a circle,
an oval and a crescent.

Look for different shapes in your house.
Make clay models of the shapes you find.

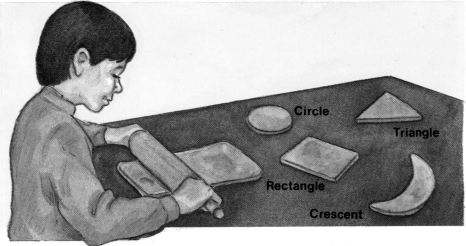

Making a jigsaw puzzle

Use a rolling pin to make a large, flat clay tile.
Cut your tile into pieces with a plastic knife.
You have made a clay jigsaw puzzle.

Put the clay pieces into a refrigerator
to cool and harden.
Mix up the pieces.
Can you or your friends fit the pieces
of your clay jigsaw back together?

Cutting slices

Roll out some clay into a cylinder shape.
Use a plastic knife to cut the cylinder into slices.
What do you notice about the shape of the slices?
Fit the slices back together to make a cylinder.

Make a solid cube.
Cut the cube into slices.
What do you notice about the shape of the slices?

Make different solid shapes.
Cut these shapes into slices.

How many balls of clay?

Make lots of small clay balls.
Try to make each ball the same size.
Put the balls together to form a cylinder.
Do not squeeze the clay balls.

Ask your friends to guess how many
balls there are in the cylinder.
How close is the nearest guess?

Clay animals

Make a model clay animal.
Can your friends guess
which animal you have made?
Try to make unusual animals.

Make twelve different-sized balls of clay.
Keep six clay balls and give six to a friend.
Take turns to add the balls of clay
to make an animal.
Try to make an ant, a dog,
an elephant and a giraffe.
Can you make any other animals or insects?

Faces and masks

Use a rolling pin to make a large, flat clay tile.
Cut your tile to make the shape of a face.
Add eyes, a nose, a mouth, ears and hair.
Make the face happy, sad, tired or angry.

Gently push the sides of the clay face.
Watch the face change its shape.

Make a mask from a clay tile.
Have you made a funny or a scarey mask?

Finger puppets

Make a soft ball of clay that will fit on your finger.
Make a face on this clay ball.
You have made a finger puppet.

Make another finger puppet to fit on to
a finger of your other hand.

Put your puppets on your fingers.
Make up a story for your finger puppets.

Making holes and craters

Roll out a thick clay tile.
Push the point of a pencil into the clay.
Push the other end of the pencil into the clay.
What do you notice?

Do the same with a large iron nail.
Which end of the nail is easier to push into the clay?

Drop small stones on to the clay.
What do you notice about
the craters made by the stones?

14

Patterns in clay

Roll out a thick clay tile.
Use a pencil and a nail to make patterns on the tile.
Make patterns in the clay with a plastic fork.

Make raised patterns by rolling
a thimble over your clay tile.
Put your fingerprints on the clay tile.

Press coins and pieces of wood
into the clay to make patterns.

Clay letters

Roll out a long clay snake.
Cut the snake into pieces with a plastic knife.
Use these pieces to make the letters of the alphabet.

Write your name using clay letters.

Make a letter.
Ask your friends to make something from clay
which starts with this letter.

16

Making a maze

Roll out a long clay snake.
Cut the snake into pieces with a plastic knife.
Place the pieces on a smooth board to make a maze.
Mark the entrance and the exit to your maze.
Make sure that there is a clear pathway from
the entrance to the exit.
Can your friends find their way through the maze?

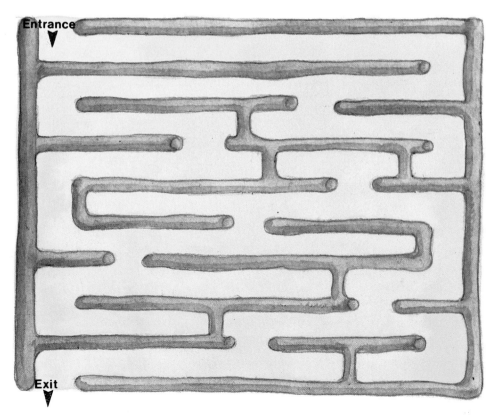

A clay map

Roll out a clay tile on a large board.
Draw a map of your street on the clay.

Make clay houses for your map.
Make model trees, street lights and traffic signs.
Place these on your map.

Can your friends guess which street
the map shows?

Clay cars

Name some cars that you know.
What do these cars look like?
Make clay models of these cars.

Make some streets for your cars to drive along.
Use long, thin pieces of clay to
show the sides of the streets.
Make clay street signs.

Place your model clay cars on your streets.

Bouncing clay balls

Make a solid ball from soft clay.
Drop your clay ball on to flat, hard ground.
Does the ball bounce?
What happens to the ball?

Now *throw* a clay ball on to the hard ground.
What happens?

Try dropping a rubber ball on to the hard ground.
What do you notice?

Does clay slide?

Find an ice cube.
Quickly make a clay cube the same size
as your ice cube.

Put both cubes on to a smooth board.

Slowly raise one end of the board.
Which cube slides first?
Feel the cubes.
What do you notice?

Making clay pots

Press your thumbs into the middle of a clay tile.
Pull up the clay with your fingers to make a pot.

Cut out a clay disc.
Make a long clay snake.
Fix one end on to the edge of the disc.
Coil your snake around the edge to make a pot.
Press the coils together to make the pot firm.

Decorate your pots.
Do your pots hold water?

Making clay boats

Does a solid ball of clay sink in water?

Form the ball of clay into
a thick-sided boat.
Does your boat float?
Make the walls of your clay boat thinner.
Does this boat float?

Make many different clay boats.
Which boats float best?

GLOSSARY

Coil To wind something round into rings.

Crater A large hole made when a heavy object drops on the ground.

Cubiod A solid shape whose six sides are all rectangles.

Cylinder A solid shape like a soup can or a roller.

Maze A set of lines or paths that twist and turn so that it is easy to lose the way.

Refrigerator A machine which keeps food and drink cold and fresh.

Thimble A cover for the end of your finger, to protect it when you are sewing.

Traffic The things which travel along the road, such as cars, lorries, buses and bicycles.

INDEX